IF I TOLD YOU

Le E. Brooks

ISBN 978-1-68526-008-8 (Paperback)
ISBN 978-1-68526-009-5 (Digital)

Covenant Books, Inc.
11661 Hwy 707
Murrells Inlet, SC 29576
www.covenantbooks.com

If I Told You

If I told you, would you believe it? If I showed you, would you receive it? What if I took you there, what if I took you where there is more than you could understand more than, you could comprehend? I just want you to know that I am God.

I remember when my wife and I went to Dallas in 2001 to the International Worship Institute. It was a weeklong conference on praise and worship, singing, and music workshops. There were prophetic encounters and much more. There were eighty-four classes, and since it was impossible to attend them all together, we split up and went to separate classes. We were overwhelmed and would over talk each other when we had a break between classes. I remember one class that I attended. It was titled Prophetic Musicianship. It was taught by Morris Chapman, a noted recording artist, renown singer/musician. He was so anointed that it was a blessing to be taught by him. He asked how many of us were songwriters. Many of us raised our hands. He said that he was a song receiver. He then explained the difference. Basically that a songwriter may be inspired to write and may start with bits and pieces of the song. This may take days, weeks, months, even years to complete. But a song receiver gets downloads and gets the whole song at once. There was a keyboard in the classroom, and he sat down and began to play and sing. He got maybe halfway through the song and stopped. He looked around the room and said, "You know, I have never heard that song before. I just received it from heaven." He then asked how many wanted to have prophetic music in their life? There were more hands raised. We all were so excited. He said a short prayer, then the class was over.

When we got home, I was at home alone a short time later. I wasn't watching TV. I wasn't listening to the radio. There wasn't any loud noise coming from outside, but I heard this music. It seemed to be coming from the middle of my chest. It was a song that I had never heard. I heard everything. I heard the music, the lyrics, the instruments, the beat—everything. I grabbed a small cassette recorder and sang into it to capture the song. As soon as the first song was over, another song would take its place. This was just what that class about prophetic musicianship was talking about. Now it was happening to me. Praise God. This kept happening every day usually in the morning between 2:00 and 5:00 a.m. This was when I would have my one-on-one with Jesus. I would be worshiping and praising Him, and I would began to hear new songs. One, two, three, four songs. This was the first time I heard five songs in session. I told my wife that this was happening, and at first, she was frightened. This was totally different prior to attending the IWI conference. Prior to this time, I had written about eight to twelve songs in my whole life. Now I was receiving that many every day. All praise to God. She said she had asked God if He was getting ready to take me home. I kept receiving songs until I had received about forty-five songs, and I received a call from my medical doctor. He informed me that my PSA was elevated. Not knowing what that meant exactly, we scheduled an appointment. The appointment was on my wife's birthday, and I wanted to postpone it, so she wouldn't have to focus on that. But she said, that's okay. After testing, my doctor diagnosed me with prostate cancer. That started me on radiation treatment daily for about eight weeks and Lupron shots monthly for about six months.

Lupron is a man-made hormone for the treatment of prostate cancer, breast cancer, etc. When the treatment modality was over, we had another appointment with my doctor. My PSA test results were lower than if I had had surgery, or even if there were no prostate. When I heard the results, I raised both hands in the doctor's office and gave God the praise. My doctor looked at me kinda funny. He then said that he didn't mind sharing the credit for the findings. Well, I know that God does use doctors, nurses, and whoever He chooses to aid in healing; He's God, but I know that He healed me because in the initial appointment, this same doctor, when he diagnosed me, gave me two to five years to live with treatment. That was in 2004, and I am writing this book now in 2019.

This was the beginning of my journey. I continued receiving songs, and when my doctor had first called me about my medical condition, there was a feeling that I had. I couldn't understand what it was. So I asked God in my prayer time. I told Him I had a question that I didn't understand. I said a short prayer and an hour later, He woke me up. He answered my question with a question. He said, "If I told you, would you believe it? If I showed you, would you receive? What if I took you there, what if I took you where there's more than you could understand, more then you could comprehend. I just want you to know that I am God."

He further said, "What if I took you to a place where there is more than you could understand, more than you could comprehend? Reach out and take it, for I have given it to you. I just want you to know that I am God."

> For God speaketh once, yea twice, yet man perceiveth it not. In a dream, in a vision of the night, when deep sleep falleth upon men, in slumberings upon the bed; then he openeth the ears of men, and sealeth their instruction. That he may withdraw man from his purpose, and hide pride from man. He keepeth back his soul from the pit, and his life from perishing by the sword. (Job 33:14–18 KJV)

So I have continued to receive songs. I have received many dreams in the night, many ideas, creative ideas. One of the first creative ideas that I received was a bicycle. I was having just a normal dream, and this bicycle appeared before me in midair. It was suspended in midair and then it started to fade. I said, "Oh Lord, don't let it go away." So it came back. The bicycle lifted up, and below it were twelve pictures of how to build it. They were like pencil sketches going from left to right. The first picture showed some of the basic parts like the handlebar, the frame part of the wheels. The second sketch was more elaborate showing more parts until the last picture was complete. It showed all of the designs except the color. When I awoke from this dream, I had the bicycle firmly implanted in my mind. I built several prototypes, got a utility patent, and worked it out. This was the start of having more adventures into the future and going back into the past as well as different races of beings. More in the following chapters.

2

Family History

My father, Alvester Brooks, was born in 1916, in Newton County, Texas. He had ten brothers and sisters. My mother, Izidie Brooks, was born in Newton County, Texas, in 1919. She had ten brothers and sisters. My mother and my father lived close to each other and knew each other as kids. They went to the same schools. Both families worked on their fields, growing vegetables and fruits and raised livestock such as cows, a horse or two, and pigs mostly for food. They would grow corn, peas, peanuts, and watermelons, as well. They used horses and buggy for transportation and would carry their produce in wagons to the mill to make flour and cornmeal. Instead of using cash, much of their payment was on the barter system. They would leave so many buckets of meal or whatever was the finished product, at the mill for payment. My parents told us it was a custom quite common then. If a family was going to butcher a hog or cow, they would invite their neighbors to come and share. When the other family had something to share, they would do the same.

My parents worked very hard to keep food on the table by working in the fields, harvesting or planting the crops. In the heat of summer, the ground would be hot. They would use a gardening tool to make a furrow to place their feet in the cooler dirt underneath. They worked from sun to sun, meaning from when it was so dark, you couldn't see in the morning to when it gets too dark to see in the evening. My father and his brothers also got into logging. They cut short logs that were used in the making of paper. My father and my mother got married when he was twenty and she was sixteen. They had their first child about two years later. Her name was Essie, and they had another daughter about two years later. Her name was Dorothy. My father and two of his brothers continued working in logging and moved from Texas to Arizona. My oldest brother Lee Vester was born, and in a couple years later, I was born.

My father followed the timber belt and moved to California. Two more children were born. Roy Edward and my youngest sister Donna Delores were born. My family settled in Redding, California, and that is where I started going to school. I attended Pine Street Elementary School for first grade; Cypress St. Elementary for second, third, and fourth grade; Magnolia St. Elementary for the fifth and sixth grade; and Sequoia Junior High for my seventh and eighth grade studies. I then attended Central Valley High School for my ninth grade through my twelfth grade and graduated. Note that I was the first African American to go through all four years and graduated from there. After high school, I attended Shasta Jr. College for two years in evening studies. My majors were real estate and business administration. Then I took on a full load of classes for one semester before moving from Redding to San Bernardino. I changed my major to psychiatry and began working at Patton State Hospital. After receiving my psychiatric technician license, I applied for a position at Langley Porter Neuropsychiatric Institute in San Francisco, California. When I was accepted, I moved to San Francisco. I began a career in the University of California as a licensed psychiatric technician. I was blessed to function in many treatment modalities. I was able to be instrumental in helping many clients deal with issues associated with alcoholism, illicit drug use, and mental crises. We were a team of clinicians involved in home visits, group intervention, crisis intervention, and group therapy. I was chosen from my team that consisted of a psychiatrist, psychologist, social workers, registered nurses, and psychiatric technicians to lead inpatient and outpatient groups. I also worked intensely with the local jail and worked with the incarcerated population around their eligibility. As audiovisual coordinator, I filmed and managed the recordings of the psychiatric seminars and supervised the usage of video equipment.

3

My Music Ministry

When I was about eight years old, I remember my parents and all my brothers and sisters and I were living in Redding, California. We attended a small Pentecostal church there. There were between two to twenty-five members maybe. I could remember that it had a woodburning potbelly heater as the only source of heat. I remember that there was a minister who played the guitar. It was such warm music. It was an electric acoustic guitar. We were so excited when we heard him play. My two brothers and I went home after church, took a pine plank, and cut the shape of a guitar. We used clear fishing line for guitar strings and nails to hold the strings in place. It didn't work very well, and my parents went and bought us a used acoustic guitar. I did not take to the guitar, but my parents later bought a used upright piano. Then I was able to pick out simple melodies. My father picked up the guitar and played some good ole gospel quartet music. That's a style of music that many black churches would sing in the south. My older brother started learning some songs, and my two brothers started singing together. Meantime, I purchased some 45 RPM records. I began to listen intently to each song and began to play what I was hearing. As time went on, when we as a family got together and had church at home. I would play for the service. I then began to play for a local church and formed my first small choir. I was able to play songs by ear. At this point, I didn't know how to read notes, but if I heard them, I could play it. When I moved to San Bernardino, California, I joined a local church. I played a Hammond organ prior to moving from Redding. When I arrived at this church and saw that it had both piano and organ, I started practicing the organ. It became my instrument of choice. The pastor asked me to play for the choir. That was a blessing, and my youngest sister Donna was asked to help direct the choir. It was so much fun. We had a weekly radio broadcast. It was very encouraging for people that I didn't know to walk up to me and say how blessed they were to hear us sing and play on the church's broadcast. While I was in San Bernardino playing the organ for a local church, my oldest brother, Lee Vester joined the Edwin Hawkins Singers as a tenor. At the time, they were in great demand due to a hit song, called "Oh Happy Day." On one of their tours, they came to San Bernardino to have a concert there. It was wonderful. To see the group and my brother. They had some great stories of their travels through Europe, Denmark, and Holland just to name a few.

I continued playing for my church's choir, and I also started a gospel singing group. We sang in a number of venues around San Bernardino, Fontana, Los Angeles, and Atladena. After four years, I was offered a new job in San Francisco.

I moved to San Francisco and started going to San Francisco Christian Center. This was the church that my family had joined years before. It was also the place where I received the Holy Spirit when I was fifteen. The Lord has blessed this place, and I have been so blessed from this beautiful church family. The pastor and his wife has become family, welcoming my family from the first time we attended the church. So upon my return to the Bay Area, I joined with San Francisco Christian Center and became active with the music depart-ment. At that time, there was a play annually around Easter called the *Singing Cross* under the direction of Sis. Bolton. It was stellar and was perfect in its depiction of the great story of Easter. I met my wife Renee on December 14, 1995. We were married October 19, 1996.

Profound Loss

Give ear to my words, O Lord, consider my meditation.

Hearken unto the voice of my cry, my King, and my God for unto thee will I pray. My voice shalt thou hear in the morning, O Lord; in the morning will I direct my prayer unto thee, and will look up. For thou art not a God that hath pleasure in wickedness: neither shall evil dwell with thee. The foolish shall not stand in thy sight: thou hatest all workers of of iniquity. Thou shalt destroy them that speak leasing: the Lord will abhor the bloody and deceitful man. But as for me, I will come into thy house in thy fear will I worship toward thy holy temple. Lead me, O lord in thy righteousness because of mine enemies; make thy way straight before my face. (Psalm 5:1–8 KJV)

Praise ye the Lord. Praise God in his sanctuary: praise him in the firmament of his power. Praise him for his mighty acts: praise him according to his excellent greatness. (Psalm 50:1–2 KJV)

Lord, who shall abide in thy tabernacle? Who shall dwell in they holy hill? (Psalm 15:1 KJV)

This time that I am experiencing, I don't know quite how to categorize it. I don't know any other way other to just say what's in my heart. I lost my wife. She is the love of my life. It was prophesied to her, by a prophetess in her church, that I was coming eight years before I knew her. It was eight years later to the day, that we met, not once but twice. We met on December 14, 1995. We got married on October 19, 1996. We just grew together. She was the one for me in every way. She was sweet, resourceful, understanding, but not just saying good things toward me; she built me up in the way that I felt that God wanted. We both loved God with all our heart. I would always kid her, even before we were married, that she was the only girl who liked to fix things like I did. When I would visit her at her apartment, if something was not fixed, I would offer to fix it. But she would say that she wanted to fix it. She was good at reading the directions first, then put things together. I prided myself on being a fix-it man. When I was at home with my dad and my brothers, we would be the ones who usually fix things.

My dad was a fix-it person. He built the homes that we lived in, a local church, and many other structures. He was a logger, and he had his tools: chainsaw, pliers, axe, metal wedges, and other things that he worked with. He was in the garage working on and with his tools. There was a wonderful smell of gasoline and exhaust fumes while he was working on his machines and filing his chains. He had a whole array of tools that he used daily in the mountains. He came up in the times when things were not easy to come by. So if he had a tool that wasn't the right size, he would take it to the grinding machine and make it fit. For instance, if he had a wrench that was too small, he would grind it to a larger size. So instead of purchasing another tool that was the right size, he would make the one he had to the right size. And that's the tool that would be in his tool sack or pouch. I am digressing here because I am remembering all of these things, how he would fix things. I enjoyed fixing things around the house. If it didn't work, I would make it to work better. I remember when we were young, my mother would give us one dollar when we went shopping with her. I would buy a toy. In my mind, I would see something that was not on the toy. So I would try to make it bigger, stronger, or faster. It might be comical now, but it wasn't then. My oldest brother got a new tricycle, I think for Christmas. It had white plastic handgrips with white tassels and white plastic pedals and seat. And the way many families did then instead of purchasing a toy for each child, the oldest child would get it first. Then it would be passed to the next child and so on. Well, I had the tricycle next. And it was missing a few things. By the time it was passed to my youngest brother, the handgrips were long gone. The pedals were just a medal rod where the pedals had once been. Most of the paint on the tricycle was gone also.

One day, I said to my youngest brother, "Do you want it to go real fast?" Now my mother had an old electric iron that was defective. So either she or my dad had removed the old electric cord and put it in a back closet. We were instructed to not to touch it, but being kids, we did. I told my little brother to put one end of the cord into the handlebars and plug the other end into the wall. Thank God that no one was touching the tricycle. I don't remember who plugged the cord into the wall. I could have been me, but it shot out the fuse. No one was hurt, thank God.

So back to fixing things. Renee enjoyed fixings things herself. So when we got married, I moved into her apartment. I brought all of my things—Hammond organ with Leslie speaker, my clothes, my shoes and everything else. It was a little tight, but it fit. Well, the apartment had everything already fixed. So, when we bought our first house a year later, we needed to do a lot of fixing things, painting remodeling, hanging drapes and curtains. I loved that little house. We would go and purchase curtain rods and rugs and other things. I was thinking that when we got home that I would be the one who would be hanging the curtain rods, curtains, drapes, etc. But she said, "I want to do it." So she got her tools; I had my tools. It wasn't a fight, not a literal fight. It was interesting how it all worked. We both enjoyed doing the same things, so we just took turns. She would do one window, then I would do one window. Or if it was a bed that had to be assembled, she would do half, and I would do the other half. Mind you now, she was excellent at reading the directions first. Many times I would put it together and have a few bolts or screws left over. In other words, I didn't completely finish the task of the appliance or whatever it was. Sometimes she would come by and point it out to me in her sweet way. I went down that path to show how compatible we were.

She loved the water. As a matter of fact, that was one of our first intense discussions. She had said that she loved walking on the beach at night alone. I immediately jumped into the protective mode, saying that I didn't think it was safe for her to be out on a beach alone at night. We compromised by agreeing that cruising was a better option. So we both love cruising and had gone on sixteen cruises during our marriage. We loved Royal Caribbean. We especially loved the change of cultures, weather, scenery, the different colors of the water, the food, the jewelry, and people. I could go on and on.

Most of our cruises have been to the Caribbean, the Southern Caribbean, the Eastern Caribbean, from Mexico to Jamaica. All of the saints: St. Martin, St. John, St. Lucas, etc. Every cruise was just a delight. We would stock up on things. She loved jewelry, and at first, I wasn't so much into jewelry. In my lifetime, I had only a couple of rings, although I always liked a good watch. In the Caribbean, there were so many selections and very unique stones of the best quality. I learned what to look for in certain stones, the four *C*s of diamonds, namely carat, cut, clarity and color.

I can remember thinking back, but the memories here are so vivid as though it were yesterday, and in a way, it is, yesterday. We both loved music. Renee played the violin. She played the piano, and she always wanted me to teach her how to play the organ. I promised her a number of times. We'd sit down together, and I would show her a few things. And somehow we'd get distracted into something else; it was just a lot of fun. There was not much focus on the Hammond organ. A couple of things she did learn, she played very well. And as a matter of fact, I wasn't envious, but it was like how did she learn that so quickly? It took me years to master that technique or that touch. It was that way with her in many things. I would show her something, and it was as though she already knew how but pretended that she didn't know. She was just a quick learner. She would watch what I would do and take it to the next level. But then she had other interests, and it didn't stay with her very long, and she was focusing on other things. It was like an exciting experience each day we were learning things. She showed me certain movies that I had heard the titles of, but I had not seen them or understood what the movies were about because that was not what I focused on. I did have my favorites like *The Time Machine* and *Star Trek*. Before this time, I had heard of them more than I had watched them. We both began to watch *Star Trek* and discovered that we liked the same characters: Captain Kirk, Spock, and Klingons. We were Trekkies.

We enjoyed science fiction a lot and watched this weekly program that had bigger-than-life animals, crabs that could eat a building, sharks that were huge, and deep-sea monsters. We knew they were not real, but it was fun to spend a free Saturday together. She also loved sci-fi and the supernatural.

In my youth, while I was still in Redding, my family was introduced to many healing evangelist. When they came to Redding or nearby areas, we would attend their services. I remember A.A. Allen. He was based in Miracle Valley, Arizona. He had a huge tent and had worldwide crusades. We as a family would attend and were so blessed by witnessing the manifestations of God's power.

5

Prophetic Dreams

One night I had a dream, and it was the first of a series of dreams on this particular subject. I first recall I was walking down a street. I think I was going to a church. It was a place that I had never been to before. But when I entered the building, I noticed that everything was covered with mud-like substance. It didn't seem to get on me when I touched anything, but even the people were covered with, what I would say was a tarry type of substance. The walls, the people, the floors—everything was covered with this stuff. And I recall the way the building was built: you enter from the rear of the building, but you are in the balcony. I remember that I was called up to play the organ. I had to walk down some stairs, navigate through some people, because it was a large crowd. And when I reached the instrument, even it was covered with this stuff. And I didn't understand what that was all about. But it wasn't the last of these particular dreams. Because later I recall, I had another dream. I would enter the dream. It could be that I am downtown, walking or whatever. Then I look around and I notice that everything is covered with blackness. This time it was totally black as though someone had poured black paint over everything. The people didn't seem to be aware of their covering, but I was. The trees, the grass, the streets, the cars, the building, the people, everything was covered with this blackness. I would just walk through, not knowing what was going on. Then

I would have one dream after another, and this was the common occurrence. I didn't understand.

Finally I had a dream I was in some building in San Francisco. I recall in this particular building, you go in the back, and there was a railing a couple feet high, about the height of a chair or a small table.

These gentlemen were sitting on this railing, and it encircled the space where I was. I was in a lower level. I noticed around their feet, there was some loose change, and I started to pick it up. A couple of them were sort of pushing my hand with their feet, keeping me away from the money. It wasn't theirs, and I don't think they saw it until I did, but that was what was happening. Then one of the gentlemen looked down at me. He said something to me. I didn't think it was significant. But I started to talk with him. And shortly after the conversation started, it was kinda like, "Who are you? Where are you from?" kinda thing. I started talking with him, but then I noticed that the blackness that was all over his skin and his clothes started to disappear, and I looked around. There were probably five gentlemen there. He was the most forward one, and he was carrying the conversation. He was a CEO of some company, which I can't remember.

The gentlemen to his immediate left was a lawyer of another firm. It seemed that all of them were some kind of businessmen. But what was so remarkable was that the blackness that was on their skin and clothes disappeared. Even the sun came out, and there was a brightness that I didn't notice before. Everything was bright, and I woke up.

*****

A short time later, I had another dream. This time I was in a prison. It was horrible; it was deplorable. In the prison, the inmates were fighting. The wardens were egging them on and making bets. They had this game where they used sharp instruments to strike each other. They seemed to have no way of escaping other than going through the antics that the wardens had them doing. But everything was black. The ceiling enclosing this space was high above, and I could see that there were some windows, but they were covered with this black dust. All this black dust was everywhere.

On the ground, there were broken pieces of concrete, and rebar, as though they had dismantled part of the building. The inmates were poorly clothed, and some didn't have shoes for their feet. But they were forced to run back and forth over the floor. Some of their feet were torn and bloody. What was most remarkable was the tarry substance covering everything. In the dream, it was so deplorable; I really wanted to wake myself up. I felt myself gradually waking up. As I did, I came to the realization. I said, "You know, I could pray while I'm in that prison." So as it would have it, I went back to sleep, and I went back into that prison. And I said, "Jesus," and it got quiet. And again, I said, "Jesus," and I noticed that a small area around me where the blackness was, went away.

A couple of the prisoners heard me, and they turned and looked at me. And I said, "Jesus, Jesus." Each time I would say that, a larger area would clear up. And then the prisoners joined in with me.

They started chanting, "Jesus, Jesus." A larger group gathered. They were all chanting, "Jesus, Jesus." The wardens started to take notice because a larger group started gathering. Up above, there were shafts of light that were breaking through the ceiling. The actual ceiling was breaking open, and shafts of sunlight came through. The areas got bigger and bigger, and the blackness was dissipating so much that the whole atmosphere changed. The prisoners gathered around, and even their torn and tattered clothing didn't look so bad anymore. You could see the color of their clothes, you could see their skin, and you could see the excitement in their eyes. And they all kept shouting and pretty soon, there was no ceiling. Birds were singing; the sunlight was beaming. The grass was so green. Everything that was so black and dreary was now so bright and cheery. Even the walls disappeared. The wardens, they were angry and upset. They left because they couldn't overcome the joy and happiness that was being exhibited there. Everything changed. In the next recollection I had, the prisoners were free. There was a bus stop there. They all were cheerfully getting on buses. There were cars. It was a beautiful area. It was a jungle setting now. But the trees were so beautiful; the grass was so bright and green. There was just such happiness in the air. The prisoners who were moaning and groaning in pain before were now kidding their buddies and patting them on the back. They were just so excited. They all seemingly had a cheerful destination to go to. I was just so excited.

I looked across the street. There was another similar building, the way this prison had once been. So in my dream, I was able to sail up in the air. I sailed over, and I was in this other prison. It was a similar scene the way the first one was. Only in this building, there were not only prisoners and prison guards, but also, there were these huge human beings. They were around thirty, forty, and fifty feet high. Some of them were like on the floor enmeshed in the ground in all of this oily, greasy substance. When I landed over there, I started, "Jesus, in the name of Jesus." I was rebuking and praising God. And all at once, here again, there were shafts of light coming through the ceiling. And there was excitement, and the blackness started to peel away from the people. These were big, huge giant of men, they were angry. They had these real growling voices. One of them was near me, his head was at least twenty feet across and he was at least fifty feet high, but I was able to sail up into the air. I saw this great and massive hand coming at me, and it was black with oil and grease. But there was a force behind me that pulled me back as the swing came, and he missed me. He swung again, and he missed again. Each time I would move back, I would say, "Jesus Jesus."

Then the chant began, "Jesus, Jesus". He was over-powered and he fell to the floor. And the blackness started to dissipate. Once again, the shafts of light came through the ceiling. The people who were inside that prison began to chant, "Jesus, Jesus."

The prisoners were set free. The blackness and oil and grease that had once covered them was no longer present. The pain and anguish that they had been experiencing was gone. And as I was waking up, they were also leaving. The walls and the whole area had changed. The atmosphere was bright and cheery. There were birds singing and the grass was green.

I came to the conclusion that the blackness, the oily, greasy, tar-like substance represented sin. But, we can be set free and delivered from sin. We just need to call on Jesus, and he will set you free.

One night, I had a dream that I entered a museum. But it wasn't a normal museum. I noticed an exhibit as I entered on my left. There was a statue. As I approached, I saw it was a statue of a Syrian god. It was probably four feet to four-and-a-half feet tall, and it was made of what looked like a green jade or some kind of green stone. It had elephant like ears, a big mouth, and eyes that were open. It had this weird expression on its face. On it's right side was this dancing girl. She had arm bracelets on both arms on her wrists. She had necklaces around her neck. She was scantily clad as though giving worship to this god. As I walked beyond the god, I noticed there poised on the side of him, all lined up, were demons. The first one I looked at, it's skin looked like leather, and it had a camel's head. I could tell it was alive. It was oblivious to my presence. I could tell each time it would take a breath, it's nostrils would flare up. It was probably seven feet tall. It was just poised there looking straight ahead. Next to it was another demon. The first one looked sort of brown skin; the next one was green. It looked like it was made of leather. It had wings, and it had a camel's head. Next to it, there was another demon. There were seven all together. They all were about the same height, about seven feet to seven-and-one-half feet tall. It had leather skin. Some had wings, some didn't. They were all poised there as though waiting for a command. They were all totally oblivious to me.

As I walked past them, they just looked straight ahead. As I walked beyond them, I looked behind me, the seven demons, above their heads was the word *demons*, no doubt what they were. I looked beyond them on the other side. And there perched on this perch was this huge bird—I don't know if it was a raven, a crow, or a vulture—but it looked like a combination of all three. It was at least eight feet tall. It was black, also oblivious to me, but it too was perched as though waiting for a command from its master. So I continued walking forward. Beyond me were three doors, and as I approached the first door, it was open, and a lion was walking around inside. Having overcome a fear in an earlier dream, I said, "Okay." I was ready to take him on. But as soon as I started walking toward the door, someone inside of it immediately closed it from the inside. The second room that I walked to, there was another lion. And once again, I approached it without fear. Someone inside closed that door as well. The third door was still open, and as I approached, I noticed inside was this big gorilla. It was at least twelve feet tall, black, and it was aware of my presence and was challenging me to come forward, his teeth bared and his claws ready. I had in my right hand what I thought was a cup of yogurt. I noticed behind this big gorilla there was a ring of keys, that it had once controlled of, but they were now on the floor. So I just marched straight ahead without any fear, and when it saw it couldn't intimidate me, it tried to be my friend and even reached and tried to take the yogurt from my hand, but I just pushed past him and moved into the other chamber where people gathered. I say people, but they seemed intellectually disabled. When they saw me, they approached me with some hesitation and apprehension. They started encircling me. One tried to reach out and grab the yogurt out of my hand. One tried to creep up behind me and took a swipe at my head. He did graze the side of my head, but kept running. I held my yogurt; some of it had spilled from the blow. I chased him into the back room and caught him. At that time, he seemed to really be a small child. At first he seemed to be a normal-sized person, but when I rebuked that spirit from him, he became a small child about a foot to a foot-and-a-half high. He still maintained the adult features but was a small image. There was no fear within me while I was going through this cave/museum. I was able to walk up to a previously locked door and open it. I had the keys, and I was able to walk out of the building.

*****

The following is a true experience that I went through. My oldest brother had been sick for a while with diabetes. He had spent a long time in and out of the hospital. The doctors were doing what they could do for him. But he didn't seem to get better. In fact, he just seem to languish and get worse. Through our prayers and fasting, and seeking God, it seemed that things remained the same. Although his spirits were high when we would visit him, it was distressing to see all the tubes attached to his body. Well, God always prepares us for what is coming if we keep our hearts sensitive to Him. So on August 7, 2008, I was at home. It was in the afternoon, shortly after two o'clock. I was feeling rather sleepy, and being retired, I was able to have the luxury to take an afternoon nap, which I did. I had no sooner gone to sleep that I felt as though I was wide awake, and I was downstairs in our family room, in our easy chair. The chair was facing down the hallway toward our bathroom, off the hallway, at the end, on the right side. I can remember, I was as awake as I am now. I don't really believe I was asleep. There was a bright light at the end of the hallway, and I focused my eyes, and I saw Jesus standing in the doorway of our bathroom. It scared me so much, I really started screaming at the top of my lungs. I saw Him. He was dressed in, the only way I could describe it was a lime color, only it had some yellow in the color. It was the top portion of His clothes, which was a shirt or more like a blouse. And He had on pants that were a darker green. But there was light emitting from the inside. Everything was aglow out of His clothes. That was the light that I saw at the end of the hallway. Light was coming from inside of His clothes. I looked through the wall, at Him. He was partially in the doorway of the bathroom. I saw His eyes; they were filled with peace and love and understanding. He didn't say anything. He stood there and smiled at me. I was so afraid, I screamed, but there was a peace coming from Him. The chair that I was in flew back. It swiveled to my left, which was toward our kitchen.

Now the ceilings there were about eight feet high. And I saw an angel over at the end of the table He was on. He actually was translucent. I could see the wall behind Him. I could see through Him, and I could see His form. He was wearing what looked like a wedding gown. It was white cloth with a lot of beautiful bows and decorations. His lips were pursed as though He was blowing something toward me. I didn't see anything; I just felt such a peace, and a reassurance and strength. I screamed again because it scared me. I was afraid but excited. I was just…I don't even know how to describe the feeling. I can't remember how long these moments lasted. In a flash, although it seemed to last a long time, they were gone. But the peace, the understanding, the knowledge, the wisdom, the love, the compassion that I felt, it built me up for what was coming next. I didn't know, but the next day exactly, close to twenty-four hours later, I lost my brother. There was not the feeling of hopelessness or helplessness. There underneath all the grief that I was feeling, the reassurance, the support that God left in my heart. And the angel, he must have blown something on me that was so warm. After my brother's death, I was able to help the rest of my family through the crisis. God knows what He is doing always. And that wasn't the end of it.

On August 8, 2008, I lost my oldest brother. On September 28, 2008, I lost my dad. The feelings and emotions that I felt when Jesus came to my house with the angel was indescribable. I don't know the angel's name. He didn't say anything. He just pursed his lips and blew something toward me. That strength kept me, and I was able to console the rest of the family.

*****

One night as I was sleeping, I saw Jesus standing in a doorway. I don't remember what building it was where I saw him, but I could see half of His figure through the doorway, and I could see His right hand extended out; and I don't know how to explain it, but I began seeing through the wall; I could see Him. And His eyes were looking at me, and He was smiling. His eyes were filled with so much warmth and love. And then I saw Him on the Cross, and He had the thorns on His head. He was on the cross, and the next thing that I remember, I was going through a tunnel. I was tumbling through a tunnel like a corkscrew. I could feel myself. I could feel the wind going past my head. I was going faster and faster and faster. And I was going counterclockwise, and it seemed like I was going back in time. And I could see a light. It looked like it was miles and miles ahead of me, but it was getting closer and closer and closer. And as I drew closer, I exited the tunnel. As I did, I looked around, and to my right was a sphinx. Was I in Egypt? To my left, I saw what looked like telephone wire stretched between poles from left to right. There was only one wire. It would go to the left, and the next one would go to the right. I was being drawn by a force; I was sailing above the ground. I was forty or fifty feet in the air, I guess. And to my left, I could see water. It looked like a shoreline. The sky looked like a steel, like steel gray. It looked like early morning; it's hard to tell. But I kept sailing, and then I felt myself being pulled into this building. And it was a red brick building. I was on the steps, and I looked down at myself. I was still in my pajamas. I had blue pajamas that were similar to a onesie that I went to sleep in. And I had a flannel kind of pajama top. And I walked up to the top, and it was a porch thing. And I looked down on the street. There were these guys, and they were standing there. They looked something like Salvation Army, some religious sect, and I didn't recognize their insignia. I asked them, "Where am I?"

I said, "Where am I? Excuse me, can someone tell me where I am? What city? Where is this?"

Finally one person looked at me, and he said, "Who are you?"

And I said, "My name is Le."

"That doesn't ring a bell."

He was looking at one of the other people, and was talking more to himself than anyone else. He said he doesn't know where he is. "When I leave the house in the morning, I know where I'm going." So they sort of chuckled and started walking away. I didn't know where I was. And then I heard some shuffling steps going up some brick concrete steps. I was in like a little room in the back. And this old lady came up the steps, and she looked in my direction really pensively.

And I said, "Look, I'm sorry, I don't know I'm leaving."

And she looked at me and said, "I don't think I like you."

And so, she walked real fast into the back, and I heard her using those old phones; you know, the ones that you wind up. She called the police. Well, they were called bobbies, and I thought, I didn't do anything. So in my state, I was able to walk onto the porch and sailed out over the street. And when I got out there, it was a beautiful, rustic city. It was all wood. The grass was pretty and green. The sun was shining so bright and pretty. I didn't see any cars, though, and I couldn't recognize where I was. As I got further, I saw a crowd of people standing near a walkway, a stairway. The stairs went down, and there was a lobby and a building in this open space. It was really an old-fashioned building, and everyone seemed to be wearing heavy clothes. And I looked at them and I was in pajamas. I looked up on the side of the hill. I could see the ground looked so rich; the grass was green. The trees were so beautiful. The soil seemed to be so rich, as though it had been fertilized. I could hear the birds singing. But I didn't know where in the world I was. So I turned to someone standing near me.

And I asked, "Where is this? Can you tell me what city this is?"

And someone said, "This is Salt Lake City."

And I asked, "What's the date?"

He looked at me as though everybody knew that and said, "This is 1929."

And then they just turned and started walking away. And I looked at their clothes, and they didn't look familiar. They looked like way, way back then old clothes. Then I heard someone calling from the back. It was the, well, they called them Bobbies.

He was calling out saying, "Hey monkey, hey monkey." He was referring to me. I looked back, and he had on a blue uniform. It had that kinda braid on the collar, his sleeves, and on his helmet and shoulders. He was running toward me with a nightstick in his hand. I was able to sail across this lobby across this open area going to this building. It looked like a castle. I actually saw two people sailing across from right to left, and the woman was wearing a long flowery dress, and the man was wearing what might be a suit. They seemed to be floating on what looked like a blue smoke. So I went into this building that looked like a castle. Inside I could see it was like I was in Britain. There was a group of men around a table. All of men had those white wigs. They were pounding on the table. They were going through some kind of political legislature procedure. I didn't know exactly what they were saying, and I just excused myself. I kept hearing this Bobbie coming behind me. He kept saying, "Hey monkey, hey monkey." I kept looking down at myself. I was so aware that I was wearing pajamas while everyone was fully dressed. There was a parade that was going on. It seemed like they were either in costume or darileks, but there was a crowd of people around them, and some of them had clothes as though they were vagrants or something. So I just joined in with them. I wasn't as obvious with my clothes being what they were. Some of their clothes were old and tattered, so I just walked in the parade with those people. When I woke up, I was in my bed.

*****

One night, I had a dream. We were in an open field. What was happening? It was like a global institution that was taking over. It presented like a big giant spiderweb. There were big black spheres floating above the ground. All these spheres were connected together with a giant spiderweb. They were as far as the eye could see, these agents. They were of all sizes and shapes and colors. They had all kinds of colors and personalities and would match with people on earth. They were super salesman and would offer all kinds of things to get people to join into this organization. For them to join this entity, they had to agree to allow this web to cover up everything. Each area that allowed the web to cover it, one by one, the people would be caught up in the web. What the whole entity was, was a network that was all going to be run by black widows. Around the fringes, those who accepted it, the web would get thicker and thicker. The spiderweb was sticky, and a person couldn't walk on it without getting stuck. You could look around and see people who were caught. Once there was a certain amount of the web, the person is stuck. People were being encouraged to take these gliders, actually balloons, that would take them up into the air. Once a person is up in the air, they lose control to move about; they have to accept what is around them. The air became filled with these webs. You could see all of these webs strings going as far as the eye could see. There were these big black spheres positioned all around. The web would thicken. If it caught you, it would roll you up in the web. Then the person is powerless, just like in a natural spider web, then you would be food for the spider. Then here would come the big spider.

We were in an area, and everyone was being encouraged to ride these glider balloons. There were so many incentives that were offered to entice people to join in. As a person would accept, there would be more and more webs added, but there were all kinds of other things that a person could have. This entity would offer riches beyond means. Your whole living experience would be so elevated and liberated. The people would float up in the air on the gliders, and have all the freedom of the air. But what it was doing was it would allow these webs strands to expand further and further. I was saying. "No, it's a trick. leave it. You don't have to accept this."

It became harder and harder to talk with people or to convince people. Those who didn't want to listen, they were able to get into this higher elevation of life. Then you would see one by one, they would get wrapped up in these strains of web, but they were incapacitated. The system wouldn't let you see those who got caught and were rolled up in the web. The system would whisk them away. And then there would be new people. We were on the top of what looked like a box car. As far as the eye could see, there were these people resisting the system but they were slowly being absorbed. And then they had what I will call greeters. These people were dedicated, totally sold out to this entity; they were coming to greet those who hadn't joined. They were going to come and be friends. Everyone was finding someone to meet with, basically to indoctrinate. A lot of these people looked really weird. Some were tall and some had all kinds of color. It was like they tried to find what you liked. This entity would try to find all kinds of people, all shapes, sizes, personalities dressed in different ways, or activities, something to connect with someone. Then that would be your person to bring into the organization of this worldwide web. I saw them coming. Some of them would just dive. They would do all these antics to impress someone, and then they would come up and say, "Oh, where can we meet? How ya doing?" They were very friendly. I was just dodging all these people. I was just ignoring them. When you ignored them, they keep trying to win you over to get your attention or admiration. Then they come over and start talking.

Finally this guy came up to me, and he said, "Hey, where can we meet?"

I looked at him, and I said, "I don't know you." And he just turned all different kinds of shades of color, trying to attract me.

Some people who were saying that they didn't want to join, they were about to commit suicide to prevent joining this organization because they knew what was coming. But it was as far as the eye could see, these things were happening. And you look up and you could see the web thickening and thickening. I was rebuking, and every time you rebuke, it would tear a hole in the web. And unless everyone would do it together, it would mend itself. Then here would come a thicker force to try to surround and cut off and ruin a person's influence in that particular area. As I was waking up, I was still resisting this force.

*****

On February 14, 2017, I had a dream that I was sailing through a building where I used to work. Only the whole building was under construction. As I was sailing down a long hallway, I met a gentleman walking. He told me that his wife called him slow. We had a casual conversation until, we parted ways. He went straight ahead. In my dream, I was looking for a restroom, so I took another corridor. I went to the end, and not finding a restroom, I returned to the main hallway. There was a tall gentleman standing in the hallway. As I approached, he asked if he could talk with me. I was in a hurry, so I asked what he wanted while continuing to move forward. He asked if I liked sweet potato pie? Then I was annoyed, and I felt myself waking up from the dream. I was still looking in his direction, and I couldn't hear what he was saying. But I could read his lips. He was saying, "You are eating the wrong foods." By this time, I was fully awake, with my eyelids closed, lying on my right side. I saw through my eyelids that the man who was in my dream was sitting by my bed, smiling at me. I felt and saw him reach out his left hand, placing his thumb on my left cheek, and his forefinger on my left eyebrow. In his right hand, he had a small lens. He looked into both of my eyes. He put the lens down and picked up an eye dropper and placed a drop of clear liquid in each eye. At this time, I opened up my eyes, and he was still sitting by my bed, grinning at me. I had to use the restroom for real, and I got up and walked down my hallway to the restroom. He walked with me part of the way and then disappeared. I felt the gift of tongues start. I have been filled with the Holy Spirit since I was fifteen and daily exercise my prayer language. The gift of tongues, as referenced in the Holy Bible, in the book of Acts 2:2., "At that time it describes one of the manifestations of being filled with the Holy Spirit, was speaking in a heavenly language, usually not known to man."

A short time later, I was sharing with my sister about my experience. When I mentioned what this angel said about the sweet potato, she got excited. She had just read about the benefits of sweet potatoes, that the sweet potato and yams has an abundance of vitamins, especially good for eyes. I was excited about the benefits of sweet potatoes since I have been diagnosed with glaucoma and have had extensive treatment over the years.

*****

My wife and I were serving at this church, we were praise-and-worship leaders. I was one of their musicians. We had served three years and felt God's leading for us to leave. We communicated this to the pastor, and with his blessing, we asked for a leave. We had removed all our stuff from the church building but my organ and speaker. So, not wanting to make a disruption in the service, I had to plan to have it removed between services. The pastor's son was getting married, so he and the pastor and a few others were going around the church pointing out what needed to be moved and how to decorate for the wedding. The son came to me and asked if I could move my organ and speaker to the storage room because he wanted to use the church platform for pictures after the wedding? I said that I would move them. We had already given the pastor our notice, and moving the organ and speaker was the last thing we had to move.

My wife Renee had heard about a seminar in Moravian Falls, North Carolina. After hearing her describe what she had read about the seminar, I was anxious to attend, so we scheduled the seminar. When we arrived, we were pleased and blessed beyond our wildest expectations. The seminar was actually a three-day conference in a beautiful setting in the mountains. It was hosted by Geary Oakes. The main speaker was Larry Randoff. Moravian Falls has a long history of angelic citing and supernatural dreams. So the first night, Renee saw a big angel in native attire.

She was about seven-and-a-half feet tall and was standing in front of the classroom, grinning at her. When she told the leader of the service, he was not surprised and said it was common to see angels and other angelic beings there. That night, I had the following dream. I was in a red Corvette SUV. I know of no such car, but there was one that night. It had a Corvette front and grill, with the word *Corvette* written across the hood. There were three rows of seats with a space behind the last row of seats with a hatchback. To exit the rear of the car, the hatchback lid was raised. Well, in the dream, I was in the space behind the third row of seats. All the other seats were filled with people. So I asked the driver to stop, and I would roll out the back door. So the driver stopped, and I rolled out the back door. I exited the car, walked around to the right side of the futuristic car, and I could see a green Corvette SUV. That was my car, and as I sailed over to it, I noticed the instrument panel. It was filled with instrumentation from one side to the other. The dream ended.

When we returned home from Moravian Falls, we returned to that church. We only had a few weeks left. So I called a group of movers for the removal of my Hammond organ and the Leslie speaker. When they arrived to move my organ, the boss of the movers said that they would take the organ out the front door because it was closer. But one of the movers said, "No I am a mover, trust me. We will roll the organ out the back door." Those were the same words in my dream, he said it again, "We will roll the organ out the back door, trust me, we will roll the organ out the back door." I couldn't contain myself. So what did they do? They rolled the organ out the back door. Just like the dream I had when I got out of the red car and got into the green car, I had said I will roll out the back door just like they rolled the organ out the back door.

Songs in the Night

To the glory of God, I thought that I would share some of the songs that I have been given. It would be difficult to give them all, so I will share parts of songs, I pray the lyrics will be a blessing.

"Give Yourself to God"

> Don't you want to live for Jesus,
> Or do you want to live in sin?
> He can make your life worthwhile,
> And give you peace within.
> Don't you want a purpose in life,
> And gain, gain, and gain,
> Or would you rather just do the same old thing?

"With Your Love"

> With Your love you,
> have brought us this far,
> With Your love,
> It's like sitting on a star.
> Looking at the massive universe,
> There's no limits to Your Love.

"God's Heavenly Rhythms"

As I walk the shore as waves ebb and flow,
As I hear the birds sing,
Then that lets me know,
That you made it all.

"There's Nobody Else"

There's nobody else, there's nobody else,
Nobody else can be found.
To pick up my burdens and pain,
Nobody else but Jesus, my Jesus, my Jesus,
Just my Jesus.

"Loving God"

Loving God, that's what I live for,
He's always doing wonderful things for me.
He's always there when I need Him most,
Loving Him fulfills my greatest desires.
Loving God, that's what I live for.

"Do You Know the Savior"

Do you know the Savior of your Soul?
Do you know the Savior of your Soul?
Do you know the Savior of your Soul?
Do you know the Savior of your Soul?

"Call Him"

Just call my Jesus and he will make you brand-new,
Call him He's waiting there for you.

"Lord You're Good"

Lord You're good, not just when things are,
But You are good, because you are.
You don't need nobody else,
But You are good all by yourself.

"I Only Let Peace and Love"

When trouble tries to come once more,
And darkness lurks nearby,
I must remind myself,
That I only let peace and joy enter in.

"Highest Praise"

Tell me what is the highest praise,
Tell me what is the highest praise,
Hallelujah.

"How Marvelous"

In the morning when the sun rises,
And the dew is still on the ground.
I look up at the trees,
And hear the birds and the bees.
Then I say, Lord how marvelous you are.

"In All Things"

Lord, I thank You for the morning,
And I thank You into the night.
And I thank You when things are going right.

IF I TOLD YOU

"We've Got a Job to Do"

We've got a job to do, we've got a job to do,
Spread good news all over the world.
We've got a job to do, we've got a job to do,
Tell every man, women, boy, and girl.
Don't let nobody stop you,
Even if they try to block your way.

"Keep Your Mind on Him"

Why don't you keep your mind,
Why don't you keep your mind,
Just keep your mind on him.

"Sing a Little Melody"

Sing a little melody about Jesus,
How he kept you,
Sing a little melody about Jesus.

"Emanuel"

Emanuel, Emanuel, Emanuel

"Joy"

What three-letter word is better than happiness,
Joy.
What three-letter word is better than happiness,
Joy.

"If I Told You"

If I told you, would you believe it,
If I showed you, would you receive it.

"That's What I Offer"

Praise, praise, that's what I offer to You,
Worship, worship, Lord, let it fall on me.
Praise, praise, that's what I offer to You.

"To You I Give All My Praise"

To You I give all of the glory,
To You I give all the praise,
For You alone deserve it,
To You I give all glory and praise.

"He Found Me"

One day when I was in sin, Jesus found me,
He picked me up and turned my life around.
Now that He has changed me and rearranged me,
He placed inside a smile where there was a frown.

"His Is the Sweetest Name I Know"

Jesus, Jesus,
His name is the sweetest name, I know.
Jesus, His name is the sweetest name I know.

"Sweeter Than a Honeycomb"

Sweeter than a honeycomb,
Lord, I love You.
Sweeter than a honeycomb,
Sweeter than the honeycomb.

"I Open Up My Heart to You"

Lord I need You,
Lord I want You,
I open up my heart to You.
Come on in, Jesus,
Lord, You are welcome.

"Thank You, Lord"

I just want to say, thank you,
For what You have done for me.
I just want to say, thank you,
For what You have done for me.

"The Lord is My Fortress"

He protects me,
From all the darkness and misery.
The Lord is my fortress, he protects,
The Lord is my fortress.

"Come Holy Spirit"

Come Holy Spirit,
Come Holy Spirit.
Reign in me,
Reign in me.

"I Have Discovered"

I have discovered,
That there's no greater love.
I have discovered,
That there's no greater peace.
I have discovered,
That there's no greater joy.

Futuristic Dreams

One night, I felt as though I was in a time when what I witnessed was not yet. I was in the city of Madrid. I approached what looked like a street. Parked near the edge of the street was a bus that had a frame with seats for passengers, no roof and was propelled by a system that was either safe fusion or fission. There were no fumes and no sound. Parked in front of it was a vehicle that was the size of a passenger car but was more like just a frame without a roof. It, too, was propelled by some kind of fusion or fission. It seemed to have the capacity to hear and converse with people on the street without microphones. As I crossed between these two vehicles, I walked down the sidewalk space. I noticed, that the people were from nine-to-twelve feet high, some really thin. The outside of two buildings were actually made up of products. The product was on the second floor and were cartoon-like characters. It was truly a display of 3D TV. All characters were outside of the typical TV box.

*****

Another dream I witnessed where there was a system of air-streams that would support people in a sitting or standing position without any visible means of any machine. There were different directions that the air highways would go. The airstreams had a number of lanes going each direction and appeared to be about two to about four hundred feet above the ground.

*****

One night, I was with someone who was more familiar with this particular. We were traveling in what seemed to be a small two-person helicopter. This system would fly above an existing highway. Their vehicles were brightly colored, like a bright red or orange. There was a row of brightly colored balloon-type markers along the route. These vehicles would fly about 150 to 200 feet above the highway and seemed to drive themselves, keeping proper distances between the vehicles ahead and behind.

*****

One night, I was in a place where there were mounds and mounds of what looked like Turkish cloth blankets. There were only two primary colors. They were a pale blue and a pale pink. When I first noticed it, the cloth was randomly spread over the ground. Upon closer inspection, I noticed there was something wound up in them. It was people. There were thousands of them. For when I saw the people, they seemed everywhere. They seemed to have no place to go, and yet the rest of the world did not seem to notice them. The streets were clogged with mounds and mounds of cloth. There was no place to stand without stepping on these blankets. As I moved about this area, I noticed that the areas had pathways that had been trodden by people traveling. When I first encountered the people who were covered with the blankets, they seemed to have no place to go and were just sitting in large numbers. I did not see anyone else talking or communicating with them. They were just ignored. I noticed that as I walked in certain areas on the sidewalk, my feet stepped on something that crunched under them. From the stench in the air and the flies, it was clear that there were people who had died and were left under the mounds of blankets. The first time I saw this area of blanket-covered people, it was overwhelming. But what was even more appalling was the fact that no one else seemed to notice.

The next time I had a dream about people covered with the pale blue-and-pink fabric, I thought about talking with them. But I did not. It seemed there was a stigma against communicating with them. I can't remember how many dreams I had about seeing the blue-and-pink cloth and the people wrapped in the blankets before I communicated with them. It was in a large city, I think San Francisco. I remember that the streets were clogged, and the busses were having trouble navigating through what were mounds and mounds of blankets. The people in them were just sitting in groups in the streets and sidewalks and even inside of stores. When I spoke to a group of men nearby, they seemed undaunted about being in the large blockage. They responded to me in a noncommitted manner.

*****

I had a dream I can't remember what city. There was something familiar, but I can't place it. Everybody I looked at was wrapped in these blankets. They were a darker color. Usually, they were red. They were striped, and they were plaid. They were full-color one-tone blankets. Many of them were the darker blues and the darker reds. I saw a lot of different colors, but no main theme color. But all these people were wrapped in the blankets, some people were living, and some were dead. It was like the living were willing to lie down with the dead. These people were everywhere, lying in these blankets. I didn't see but a few people walking around. When I say a few, maybe four or five at any given time. But everywhere else, the blankets were piled up in some places three and four feet high, and I'm walking on them. Every once in a while, I would step on them because it was the floor. I would hear the crunch of dead bones in the blankets. There was the stench and flies. Then I would see people inside of the blankets. I could see part of their heads; they were alive. Most of them were covered up with these blankets. I even got close, and I asked, "Why were they down on the floor in the blankets?" And they just sort of shook their heads, and as if they were saying "I don't know." It was just that the whole city seemed to be covered with these people covered in blankets, and I remember walking up a hill in the mud. I was the first person to make a track here. Seemed like everything had slid from the top of the mountain, down into the lower part of the hill or valley, and the mud was, I'd say several feet thick. In my dream, I was able to basically fly above, and once in a while, my feet might touch the ground, but I was aware of this area of this slick, slimy mud consistency on the ground.

*****

One night I had a dream. I was on a small island. There was someone with me. I can't remember who it was. As we stood near the water's edge, I noticed a lifeboat approaching. It was painted with bright yellow-and-red colors and was towing a small lifeboat behind it. The large lifeboat stopped in front of us, and I was told to get on the small lifeboat. The water was turbulent, and there were a lot of big waves. I hesitated to move into the water. But the captain of the lifeboat became more insistent. He said, Get on now." So I entered the water, and as soon as I wrapped myself around the small lifeboat, the large lifeboat took off full speed. I was being pulled by the big boat, and at times, I was underwater. I was pulled for quite a while through unfamiliar territory. There were many dark and ominous objects that I passed through. I was not allowed to go to them because the boat was pulling me through the area. After that, the lifeboat took an abrupt right turn and stopped. This was near the shoreline, and I was thrown on the shore due to the force while being pulled. When I landed, there was a force behind me, leading me forward to a building I had never seen.

When I got to the entrance, I noticed that it was a hospital. There were patients on the floor, covered in blankets, and there were flies everywhere. The stench of death was heavy in the air. I looked around and saw only a few staff members and nurses. They were definitely overwhelmed with the abundance of sick and dying patients, and they barely gave me a glance as they scurried about the rooms. I was again led by a force to go down a long hall-like room. I went to the back of the room. There I saw even a more deplorable scene. There were no beds but tables. Each had patients, wrapped in blankets. Many were dead, and I was so moved with compassion. I started calling on the name of Jesus, I went from table to table and spoke directly to the patients, even the ones that I knew were dead. I commanded them in the name of Jesus to get up and be healed. I kept speaking to the bodies on the tables then to the bodies that were floating in the filthy water. Other bodies were lying exposed to the sun and in all degrees of decay. In my dream, I was wearing some sea turtle cowboy boots that I had purchased on a cruise. In the area that I was walking, the mud and filth had covered my boots. I didn't care. I began to pray for the conditions to change.

In the dream, the dead bodies came back to life, were healthy; and after, they had new clothes. Then I woke up. It began to happen. There was movement, and the patients who were under the blankets, did stir. Some got up and then more. I felt more confidence and spoke more direct, and more patients did get up, and before long, the tables were empty as the patients got up and expressed their gratitude. I started to wall back toward the front of the hospital. As I got near the front door, I saw the staff where I had left them. Now they were excited and were ministering to the newly healed patients. I noticed that there was a side door, and when I went out there, it was awful. There was a large pond. It looked like an open sewage system, and there was garbage, broken furniture, as though it was the dumpsite for the hospital facility. Mixed with the garbage were bodies as though to be disposed with all of the rest of the broken things. I noticed one person was not yet dead and was partially submerged in the filthy water. I went over to him and attempted to retrieve him from the water, and I was also praying for God to heal him. He responded and I could see new color come into his skin. He was still physically dirty, and I helped him get into some different clothes. Then I noticed other submerged bodies and attempted to rescue them. I remember several staff members coming out of the hospital and offering their assistance. As I was waking up, there were only a few patients who we're left in their former state. Most of the other patients were either completely healed or well on their way to recovery. All praise to God.

8

Jesus Angels and Other Beings

And it came to pass, when men began to multiply on the face of the earth, and daughters were born unto them, that the sons of God saw the daughters of men that they were fair; and they took them wives of all which they chose. And the Lord said, My spirit shall not always strive with man, for that he also is flesh: yet his days shall be an hundred and twenty years. There were giants in the earth in those days; and also after that, when the sons of God came in unto the daughters of men, and they bare children to them, the same became mighty men which were of old, men of renown. (Genesis 6:1–4 KJV)

Bless the Lord, ye his angels, that excel in strength, that do his commandments, hearkening unto the voice of his word. Bless ye the Lord, all ye his hosts; ye ministers of his, that do his pleasure. (Psalm 103:20–21 KJV)

Bless the Lord, O my soul. O Lord my God, thou are very great; thou art clothed with honor and majesty. How coverest thyself with light as with a garment: who stretchest out the heavens like a curtain: (Psalm 104:1–2 KJV)

And of the angels he saith, Who maketh his angels spirits, and his ministers a flame of fire; Are they not all ministering spirits, sent forth to minister for them who shall be heirs of salvation? (Hebrews 1:7; Hebrews 1:14 KJV)

Who maketh his angels spirits; his ministers a flaming fire. (Psalm 104:4 KJV)

My wife, Renee and I attended a service where Mario Murillo was ministering. When he ministered to the congregation, the spirit of the Lord was high; people throughout the building were being blessed and healed. Several people were blowing the shofar as music was being played softly in the background. He started walking toward us. And He said, "I've got to stop all of this just long enough to let you know that people are being healed all over this room." Then he said, "My precious sister, take your hand and lay it over the cross on his chest." He was referring to me. I was wearing a silver cross with a chain. Then he said, "That man is being healed by the power of God." He said in prayer, "The Lord said I have a work for you to do. Your years are not going to be diminished. Your weakness in not going to replace your vision. God told you, you would be like Lazarus. Raise your body up from weakness and pain and give you a fresh beginning. You've got a work to do, brother. There's something you're supposed to do and you're going to do it. And you're going to finish your course with joy."

A short time later, I had a dream. I was between sleep and being awake, twilight state, and an angel came on my left side and said, "God has something for you to do."

I asked him, "What is it?"

He said, "I don't know," and then he walked about two or three steps ahead of me and disappeared.

Again I was in a dreamlike state, and another angel came from behind me on my left side and said, "There's something that God wants you to do."

And I asked him, "What?"

He said, "I don't know." Then he walked a few steps ahead of me and twirled in a half circle and vanished.

*****

One night I was in a building. I can't remember which building. But I saw this person dressed in scrubs, like the ones that doctors wear for surgery, etc. He brushed past me. I had a knowing that his name was Michael. I called him because I had a question for him. He was in a hurry, but he paused momentarily, turning in my direction. But before I could get my question together, he vanished before my eyes. One night, I was in a building like a hospital. I had, in real life, worked with a person named Jim. When I saw this other person, I thought it was Jim. Only this person was much taller than Jim. But he responded to my call. On a small table nearby, there were two packages of breath mints. One was called Ten Commandments. I can't remember what the other package said, but I picked them both up and stuck them in my shirt pocket. This big tall person retrieved the breath mints while responding to me calling him. I asked if he remembered me. He looked at me and started to deliver a message to me. He said he was in heaven; in a meeting and that it was about me. While he was talking to me, there was a person. I thought he was trying to distract me from hearing the message. His voice sounded like a bee buzzing. I was polite at first, asking him to excuse me, so I could get my message. But he even got more persistent and even moved his head directly in front of the messenger, the angel kept talking as though there were no distraction. I finally got truly annoyed with this person, which was a demon in my way, and I raised one hand in his direction and said, "In the name of Jesus," and this spirit fell to the ground.

By that time, the angel had finished his message to me, and he asked. "Did you get the message?" I didn't get it due to the distraction. Then the angel disappeared.

*****

One night, I went to an eye appointment in my dream. When I arrived at my appointment, God was my ophthalmologist. He was wearing medical scrubs, and He had on a big mirror above His head. It reminded me of a character named Marcus Welby, MD., when God examined my eyes, He found nothing wrong with them. He even let me look into the big mirror over His head. I didn't see anything wrong either.

*****

I would like to share an experience with you. And I hope that this experience will encourage you to seek God in your daily walk. Sometime ago, my wife and I, we were looking for a church home. It was Sunday, and we had visited a church we had known. Afterward we stopped at a restaurant to have a bite to eat. On my way to the restroom to freshen up, I inadvertently bumped into a gentleman who was passing behind me. He was dressed like a minister, and we both were heading the same way at that moment, and when we arrived at the restroom, we introduced ourselves. He was a pastor of a local church. So he invited us, and we did attend on the following Sunday. When we arrived, and after church had started, the music was going good, and the choir was getting ready to sing. We had seated ourselves in the congregation. He got up and said, "You know, I met someone at a restaurant last Sunday," and he went on and described the episode. He asked my wife and I to stand and introduced us to the church. They were very gracious. Afterward, some of the leaders of the church came. They invited us to dinner. They wanted to know more about us, and when they found out that we were into music and praise and worship, they invited us to join them and even in rehearsal, they asked if we wanted to join the praise team. And we thought that was nice since we were between churches at the time. We were looking for a place to worship. So we consented to attend a rehearsal, and we did and things went well. We attended one Sunday and then another. But there was something that was disturbing to my wife, more so than to me. Because I was looking at a big Hammond organ sitting up there, and no one was playing it. I was hoping, wow, maybe that's what I should be doing. I was invited and so I was excited in that way.

But during the service sermon, the minister had misquoted a couple of scriptures, and my wife was constantly digging in her Bible and she was saying, "It doesn't say that. That's not quite what it meant," whispering in my ear. And I was intent on looking at that organ, listening to the music. It seemed that she was disturbing my peace for the moment. I just wanted to enjoy the service, if you know what I mean. But God had His own plan. So it was another scripture that wasn't appropriately applied, and I heard it, but I thought, Well, maybe he meant, you know how we do. Well after service, we went home that day. It was around the Christmas season, and there were a series of rehearsals that the choir was working on for Christmas, and they had given us a cassette tape for me to learn the songs, which I was working on, and I did. But there were some troubling thoughts or feelings that my wife had. She told me later that God had whispered in her heart, but she wanted me to know what she was feeling.

So she told God, "You tell him, he is the head of this house", because she thought something wasn't right. Well, God did.

I had a dream. I was asleep, and if I can explain to you just briefly, sometimes I'm in a very deep, deep, deep sleep. But then I will wake up from a deep, deep sleep. And then I'm in what I call a twilight state. I'm not awake, but I'm not in a deep, deep sleep. Well, in that state I had this dream. In this dream, I was somewhere in San Francisco. I was near Mission Street, and there was this lady. She had a spear. She was standing on the steps of this house. As I walked up to her, she looked in my direction. I asked if I could be of any assistance. She said she was looking for someone. In her right hand, she had what appeared to be a spear, and she wasn't looking in my direction; she was looking across the street. It was a park or something there.

And without any warning or anything else, she turned in my direction and hurled that spear at me, and it hit me in the chest right in the center. Well, in the dream there was no pain, but the head of the spear sunk into my chest several inches. And it not only startled me, but it made me angry because I hadn't done anything.

So I said, "Why did you do that?" She jumped from the stairs and started running up the street about two houses up, on the same side of the street. She faced me again, and this time, she had groups of spears in her hands. She started to hurl them at me. They were in groups of about five or seven, and I could just see lights coming toward me. The first ones were like the color of green. And I was able to throw my hands up and knock them away, and here would come another group, and they were of like a yellow color. I knocked those away. Then here came another group. They were kind of a reddish color, and I knocked those away. It reminded me of the scripture where it talked about the fiery darts. She looked at me and then she said, "Well, I'm going to get the big guns." She turned and went into the place she had been standing in front of. And I turned and walked away. I was walking toward Mission Street, and I had only walked a few steps when the dream changed. Then I was walking in a large lobby of a hotel. Walking toward me were five women in habits. They were all dressed in a black habit, like nuns would wear, but their faces were like the dirt, like if you went outside and made a mud cake and just put it on your face. It was on all five of them. They walked past me without giving me a glance. I was aware of their presence. There was something ominous about all five of them. Well, behind them were three other gentlemen coming. The first one, they all had black habits. The first one, his face looked like the five who just walked past me. He didn't look at me, but the one behind him, his face looked just like a skeleton, only with a thin layer of skin. I could see the bone structure and all of that. He, too, was looking straight ahead, and he walked past me. Well, the last person in the procession was the dignitary, the higher position was in the rear. This was a procession of people walking for this particular person. His appearance was so ominous, his head was that of a skeleton. There was no skin or anything. I could see the eyes sitting in the sockets. He walked past me while not looking at me. He had the look of death. And then the dream changed again. We were at a picnic, my wife and I and some of the members of this particular church, that we had been invited to earlier. They were serving hot dogs and some type of soft drink. Well, it really wasn't a soft drink. I didn't know that. But my wife was looking at the bottle, and it had, I think they call them hard cider or something like that. I don't drink that kind of stuff, but in the dream, I thought it was just apple juice. My wife was saying, "Baby, this has something else in it. And the hot dogs were just buns. They didn't have any meat in them." And here again, I was irritated because I just wanted to have a picnic, eat my food and relax, so I turned and started to walk away from my wife. And at that time, she was lying on the floor or ground. She had her right hand extended. It caught my right ankle and prevented me from going forward. Well, a few feet ahead of me were three steps. The first step going down had a pit in the center of it about a foot wide and a foot deep. The second step had a pit in the center of it about four feet wide and four feet deep. The third step, it just went off into an abyss. At first I didn't notice it. But when I looked at it and I started walking toward it, I noticed I couldn't see anything beyond it, but I could see a mountain in the distance. In other words, I would be just walking off a cliff, but my wife stopped me. What that meant to me was God was saying, "Look out. This is not where I want you to be." So when I woke up, I explained this to my wife. And she agreed.

She said, "God had showed me, and I asked Him to show you since you are the head of the house." My encouragement to anyone hearing this is God does speak through dreams, and I know beyond a shadow of doubt that it was a warning for us not to follow that path. And we didn't, so thank God.

God met me in prayer today. In my morning prayer, I started praying in my heavenly language. He came in, and I felt as if I was lifted off the floor. I felt so overwhelmed with His glory. I could hardly breathe. I could only open my mouth to inhale. I couldn't use my nostrils to breathe. It was just so powerful, and thank You, God, for lifting me up. Then I went into a prayer language that sounded like Japanese, it was just so glorious. Then I felt an overwhelming feeling that burst into laughter. I just felt so elated, I felt blessed. I felt clean from the inside out. It was like I had been restored and revitalized. Just fresh and clean, squeaky clean. Thank You, God. Thank You, Jesus. I give You all the glory.

Hobbies

From my early childhood, I was always fascinated with water. I can remember when my parents would take us, the whole family, fishing; it was magical. We would go to some of the neatest places, and to wake up early in the morning and arrive at the lake or stream was so exciting. I remember getting my first spinning reel and rod. It was just a toy, but in my head, I envisioned catching the largest fish in the world. My parents were so patient with me, showing me how to put everything together. They would put on the line, the hook, the weight and the bobber. Then they would bait my hook. I would try to cast it out into the water, only to snag my line onto a nearby tree. I would break off the line. Eventually, I got the hang of things and was a fisherman for life. I have many vivid memories of catching that elusive fish, and of course, the biggest ones got away. Many times, we would go fishing with my mother, when Dad had to work. I would sit near my mother and watch everything that she would do. She would always catch more fish than everybody, except my dad. I had contest with my brothers. Sometimes my uncles would go with us when my dad and brothers were going to a special fishing spot. One uncle, we called him Uncle Sonny, he was always so comical and would be joking around. But it seemed that he always knew of a private lake where he had permission to fish. I can still remember the sight and sounds of that special spot. We would always seem to catch a lot of fish there.

I guess sports and music were the next things that I enjoyed doing. Although, I never got that involved with sports other than just playing at school, it all seemed so natural, and I don't remember attempting to make it a career. I just played baseball and football, tetherball, and basketball at school during PE mostly. I didn't go out for the team, although I did get a lot of pressure from my PE coach around this. During my high school years was the only time that I actually did think what would happen if I did try out for the team. My dad was against my playing, afraid that I might get hurt and then not be able to work on a job. As I'm writing this, I do remember the struggle even more stronger than I had first imagined. I was quite athletic and played well during the regular PE periods at school. I even remember being penalized by my coach for not participating. I'm sure it was not legal for him to lower my grade for that. But during that time, I didn't say anything to the school counselors. So, now many years later, I am remembering how it felt to be singled out because of it.

I guess my greatest hobby, if I can call it that, is playing music. This is second to being a true servant and worshiper of Jesus. Actually, music is one of the greatest ways of expressing my love for God. In His word, there were thousands of ways to sing and give Him praise, and the benefits are unlimited. When I first started to play, actually before I could play, we had a minister who played the guitar. The whole family loved the way that he played. So that was my start into music. But guitar was not my instrument of choice. It was when my parents got us an upright piano. I kept trying to play, and it just opened a new dimension for me. Another hobby that I have had so many experiences with is hunting. My parents, from when they were young, saw the importance of bringing food home to their families. My dad was a marksman, and he on one occasion, took his .22, and with fifty bullets, killed forty-five birds. When he was coming up, this was not a sport but survival. So we, my dad and my brothers, would go after deer, squirrels, rabbits, etc. This was for food; we would not waste anything. But the most meaningful thing was the time that we spent together, bonding together. I have many great memories of waking up early in the morning and driving to the mountains to hunt. There was something that I didn't realize until much later about my dad. He had an accident when he was young. I don't know the age he was when it happened. But he was poked in his left eye. I say poked, but his left eye was injured. We, the children, didn't know this because it happened before we were born. My dad was a marksman and did everything without showing any signs of any eye trouble. Later in life, when he was about eighty-nine, he had cataract surgery in both eyes. His vision was restored to twenty-twenty for the rest of his life. He died when he was ninety-three.

Another fascination that I had was bicycles. I can remember, I would attempt to make toys with wheels. One Christmas, my parents bought four bicycles for me, my two brothers, and my youngest sister. It was my favorite Christmas ever. My dad helped us learn to ride by running along with us while holding the bicycle. He would then let go, and we didn't know it. When I finally did learn, I felt such freedom and power that now I could go anywhere. We lived on a hill, and our house was the last house on the street. It was like a green belt for miles. It was like having our own world. We could ride for miles on the paths and traveled roads, and rarely, if ever, see anyone else. Later we started riding our bicycles to school. It was such fun; we really felt freedom, as though we could go anywhere now. It was a different time. I don't remember any real issues of theft of bicycles, although it did happen occasionally.

My fascination for bicycles led me and my brothers to many journeys. We would name certain areas that we biked. We found an old rusty truck muffler and called that spot Truck Stop. My younger brother and I were racing and had a collision. We were not hurt, but there was some damage to our bicycles. And since we both fell off our bicycles, we called that spot Roy Fell Off. Even as I write about this, it brought back many fond memories. We had so many other experiences about that time in our lives, and although it was years ago now, the memories are still fresh. I remember that we were on our bikes every day, riding and experiencing with minor augmentations, such as clipping baseball cards on the spokes to make that *clap clap clap* sound when the wheels moved. It wasn't until years later after attending the IWI seminar in Moravian Falls that I was given the vision of a completely new bicycle. I mentioned this before; the pencil sketches showed a shaft-driven bicycle with automatic transmission. It would shift itself. There was a completely new braking system. This system stores friction energy and can be accessed later to aid in moving the bicycle forward. See the chapter on creative ideas.

10

Living in the Bay Area

As I mentioned in an earlier chapter, I was raised in Redding, California. While in Redding, my brothers and sisters had many conversations about wanting to live in the city with the bright lights, social activities, exciting places to go, and people to meet. We complained a lot about not having many or any Afro Americans to socialize with. I personally remember many weekends where I wanted to go out but didn't have someone to go out with. My parents were very understanding. Dad was a hard worker, but when my oldest sister went to San Francisco for a visit, well, it all changed. She came back with some of the most wonderful stories. We all were so excited about the activities there that we planned to go to San Francisco. My sister had by then moved to San Francisco and had established herself in a large church. When we paid her a visit, it was so exciting to see all the sites for the first time. The city was bustling with activities— cars, busses, trolley cars, people, people, people. The first visit was only for a day. My parents sacrificed the most.

My dad worked in the mountains the day before we left for San Francisco. And he was the main driver. My mother had started about two weeks before, making clothes for herself, my sisters, and even made sure that we—my two brothers, my dad, and I—had our clothes together. She cut each of our hair and fixed my sister's hair. Then she baked a turkey with all of the fixings. She fried chickens, made tea cakes, chocolate cakes, lemon cake, sweet potato pies, and many other vegetables like turnip greens, etc. We left Redding around midnight Saturday. Dad drove the 337 miles. We arrived Sunday morning, just in time to go to the church's early service. When church service ended around one o'clock in the afternoon, my sister wanted us to see all of San Francisco. Of course, it was impossible. But we did get to see as much as we could. We returned to church that evening after eating and meeting so many sweet people. Sunday night after the six o'clock service, we started back to Redding. My dad had not had any rest, neither had my mother, and so the trip back home was really a test of endurance. We all were so filled with excitement and glad to have made the trip to San Francisco. I guess the adrenaline kept us going while we were there and busy with the activities. But when we got on the road, everyone was sleepy. But my dad, although very tired, had to drive. I remember that all of the family was asleep except for my dad. Of course, my mother would nod, and then wake to ask how my dad was doing. I know I took a nap but somehow felt a responsibility to stay awake. I remember when we were a short distance from home, Dad called my brothers by name to get out of the warm car and open the gate in our driveway. My brothers were sound asleep, so my dad called me. I was awake, and I got out to open up the gate. This was to become a pattern. I can remember later that my brothers would pretend to be asleep and I would respond to my dad's call and open the gate. In retrospect, I didn't mind so much. But I have so much respect for my dad and mother to have persevered to allow us to experience those precious moments. When we first went to San Francisco, I was too young to drive. But a few years later, when I had my driver's license, I volunteered to drive to San Francisco.

I moved from Redding on to San Bernardino for four years. Then I lived in the Bay Area. When I moved to the city, I discovered a number of things that I was not aware of before. When I was in Redding, I thought that I was behind the times and that everything in the large cities were sophisticated and everyone was knowledgeable about a lot of things. But what I discovered was that people were just people. There were things that were foreign to me that they knew.

But there were lots of things that were foreign to them that I knew. I remember one of our neighbors in Redding had some of his friends come up to Redding from the Bay Area. My neighbor's father asked the ones visiting from the city if they knew where electricity came from. They didn't know but said electricity came from the outlet. My neighbor and his father took them to Shasta Dam and gave them a tour of the hydroelectric plant. It was a real eye-opener. I had a similar experience with friends who had come up to visit us while we were living in Redding.

As I am writing this, I am reminiscing about how we got to Redding. I mentioned that my father was a logger before he left Texas, and so when he came to Redding, we all lived in the mountains. It was in a small logging camp, called The Deschutes Camp. It consisted of about eight or nine small cabins that were racially divided. My family which consisted of six members at the time, my parents and four small children. There was a shop to repair, weld, and maintain the heavy equipment, such as the logging trucks, the various bulldozers, etc. There was a small grocery store and a small one-room school. I can't remember the size of our cabin, but it couldn't have had more than two bedrooms. But I do remember the potbellied woodstove/heater that was the only source of heat. Although I was quite young, I remember the wintertime when the snow was piled up against the front door. Dad kept a shovel near the door. When he opened the door in the winter, he had to shovel the snow away from the house in order to get out. We as kids would look out the window at the snow laden trees. We would play a game that when the sun came out from behind the clouds, we tried to guess which tree would dump the snow from its branches and send it cascading to the ground. I remember when we as a family would drive the thirty miles or so to the city of Redding for groceries. Sometimes we would get to go to watch a movie in the outdoor movie theater. My mother did not care for going to the shoot'm ups; most of the movies were westerns. But my dad did, and we loved the popcorn.

A few years later, my family bought five lots in the city of Redding. The property was on top of a hill with a wonderful view of the city. My dad had the land landscaped with a bulldozer and built a house on it. We moved from the Deschutes Camp to the new house. In a few years, the first house was too small, with two new additions to the family. Mom had Roy, my youngest brother and Donna, my youngest sister. That brought the total family to eight. So, Dad built a larger home on the property. It had four bedrooms, one bath, a larger living room, dining room, and a small kitchen. We stayed in this house until I was in the eighth grade. My father then purchased about nineteen acres outside the city limits. He built an even larger home, consisting of five bedrooms, two-story, three bathrooms, a large living room, a large dining room, a kitchen, and a family room surrounding a double fireplace. We fenced in the property and raised livestock. We had cows, pigs, chickens, and rabbits; and Mom always had at least two large vegetable gardens. We also had about twenty or more fruit trees which included apples, plums, pears, walnuts, both english and black walnuts, figs and apricots. My dad had a well drilled since we were outside the reach of city of Redding's water system.

The day before the well was to be drilled, my parents had heard of someone who could tell where the water was, and she did come onto the property. She had a long metal pole. She held it similar to a fishing rod. As she walked across the property, the pole began to bend up and down. It continued bending with stronger velocity, then she stopped. She told my parents how deep they needed to dig and where. She said that they would hit water at about 25 feet. But she said that would be just rainwater. She suggested that that water be capped off from the well. But she said that if we drill down to about 110 feet, that there would be plenty of water. She said the stream would be about 300 feet wide and about 100 feet deep. So my parents employed a well-drilling service. When he got down to 25 feet, he hit water, just like the woman had said. So he capped that water off from the well by putting a casing in place. When he got to 108 feet, he hit the mainstream, just like the woman had said. She was off only by two feet. The water's force was so great, it came almost to the top of the well's mouth. The well was drilled in 1955. There was plenty of water for all of the years that we lived on the property until we sold it in 2018.

I can remember after I and my brothers and sisters, had moved away from Redding, my parents were the only ones living on the property. My mother had a stroke, and we all came back home. My mother was no longer able to do all of the things that she had been doing. So my older sister Dorothy took an early retirement and moved back to Redding to care for my mother. She stayed in Redding until my mother passed on July 12, 2001. My sister stayed in Redding and changed her focus from caring for my mother to caring for my dad. During this time, there was a large forest fire nearby the property. It continued to spread until the forest service firemen came to the house telling them they had to pack up and leave. The fire was across the street and headed towards the property. My sister and my dad were evacuated from the property. I received a call from them, and they informed me and my wife Renee of what was happening. They had to leave the property but were able to view from a distance what was happening. My wife and I joined in prayer for the fire to not cause damage to the home. This was a miracle. The fire was heading straight to the home. It crosses the street in front of the home and got within twenty feet from it. The fire then made a circle around the house, didn't touch any part of the house. The fire continued in a circle around the house toward the back of the house where there was a garden. The fire went into the garden and then went straight away from the house across the back of the property.

We were living in Antioch, California, at the time. On the next weekend, we came up to Redding. I measured where the fire had burned. The distance to the house was twenty feet; it didn't touch the house. My wife and I would visit my sister and Dad frequently, and each time we visited, we would like to take pictures of the orbs that would be in one place, and then if we take the same picture again moments later, there might be none. For those who may not know about orbs, they are objects that appear in the frames of pictures taken. Sometimes they are more visible at night. They may appear as clear bubbles or in many colors. Some appear to contain various objects. They are thought to be of a supernatural nature. They do make pretty pictures, and we were just impressed that some places has thousands and then they seem to move elsewhere. Saying all of this, it was fascinating that so many orbs would appear around my parent's home. Well, my sister continued to live with my dad until his death on September 28, 2008. My sister had a stroke December 23, 2015. The property was then vacant. My sister had to be moved to a care facility for treatment due to her stroke. The property, although vacant, there were no break-ins or intruders until about seven months after I had this dream.

In this dream, I was in the house alone at night. I was sailing through the house in a circular pattern down the main hallway, turned right, and sailed through the living room, through the family room, down the main hallway, turned right, and sailed through the living room again. When I was in the living room, I heard some music, and I saw a float made of festive-type balloons coming down the hallway coming into the living room. The house was built differently in my dream. The ceilings in real life are about seven feet, maybe four inches high. In my dream, they were about twelve to fourteen feet high. I noticed this geisha girl with her head near the ceiling and dressed in a short black skirt with white petty coat under her short black skirt. Her legs were about twelve feet long, and they were covered with black lace stockings with black high-heeled shoes or boots. Her face was painted with white paint, and her eyes and face had bold black markings or decorations. Her lips were painted with a bright-pink lipstick. I asked her if she knew Jesus. She was suddenly annoyed and refused to respond. I asked her again, and then I noticed another figure. This was of a man. He was even taller than she was. He had on a fashionable festive dinner jacket, with a white ruffled shirt, matching trousers and black boots. I asked him the same question: Do you know Jesus? He turned in my direction with a frown on his face, and he said, "I'm not going to take this." He reached into his pocket and pulled out a small pistol and fired one shot at me.

In my dream, I could see the bullet coming toward me, and I said, "You can't hurt me with that." I woke up unharmed. The same week the property began to be vandalized. It seemed almost every week beyond that night that we had to call the police about someone taking things from the house. I called the fire department, and they came out boarded up the windows and doors. We had already installed locks at the gates. The locks and chains were cut numerous times. The perimeter gates were broken down, etc. We decided to sell the property. I had two dreams before we sold the property. The first dream was May 7, 2018. I had a dream that our house was on fire. In the dream I said it wasn't a house that we were living in, and it wasn't this house, meaning my present home address, so it could have been the property because in the dream, the whole section burned. The second dream was on June 7, 2018. In that dream, I was in the house on the property, and the house started to come apart and eventually fell apart. In real life, both things happened. We sold the property in June, escrow closed June 21, 2018. The property was part of the highly-publicized Carr Fire in July of 2018. As a matter of fact, it was part of the first part of the Carr Fire, it was called a "fire-nado", the whole section burned, just like in my dream. Coincidence? I don't think so. I believe that God warned the family that the fire was coming. I recalled the first fire that came toward the property in 2007, I believe it was prevented due to our declaration in prayer. Now back to living in the Bay Area.

When we left Redding in the winter of 1965, my parents, my brother Roy, my youngest sister Donna, and I moved to San Bernardino, California. I stayed there for about four years, then moved to San Francisco, California. I had two older sisters, Essie and Dorothy, and my older brother, Lee Vester, living there already. It was really nice seeing them. My two sisters were members of one church, San Francisco Christian Center, and my brother was a member of Ephesians Church of God in Christ (COGIC) in Berkeley, California. So I would spend time at both places. It was so exciting, going to all of the new places like: the beach, Golden Gate Park, Golden Gate Bridge, and so many other historical sites. I especially enjoyed meeting all the new people and attending all of the musicals. I joined San Francisco Christian Center and was active in their music department. I became a member of a singing group called the Hosanna's. It consisted of about seven members. Each of us played at least one instrument, and we had hours and hours of rehearsals before being ready to sing. I have many fond memories of our singing functions, most in and around the Bay Area. I remember that we had either four or five choirs in the church. It was so much fun coming to each Sunday morning service to hear such good singing and the pastor sharing his heart to the congregation. Sharing what God had given him. We were so blessed to have benefitted from such anointed teaching, preaching, and fellowship.

Meanwhile, my older brother, Lee Vester, had joined with not one but two singing groups. He joined the choir at Ephesians long ago. Now he was in the Praisers of God led by Walter Hawkins. Then he joined the Edwin Hawkins Singers. When they came out with the hit song "Oh Happy Day," it became a growing phenomenon for gospel music. I remember so many services when they were the main group in the largest auditoriums and church venues. I remember tagging along with them, and although I didn't sing with them, it was fun to be in the exciting atmosphere in and around the concerts. I was always so proud of my brother to see him on stage and hear about the many stories of the group's travel, etc. Earlier in the book, I talked about my job and duties around that. But what I didn't mention was my love for the fishing areas. I was new to saltwater fishing, so I met a brother at the church and we went fishing a lot. So we teamed up. Did I have a lot to learn? The first thing I learned was that you never turn your back to the water, for the waves are always coming in, but they are not the same size. One may come up to your ankle and the next one could be up over your shoulders. And if you are not looking, it could sweep you off the place you may be standing. I did learn to watch the tides, etc. We caught some really pretty fish: perch, sand dabs, flounders, and striped bass. We caught king fish, crab, and several kind of rock cod. Once I got the hang of things, I would visit some of the safer places after work. Where I worked at the UC campus, I could take the long way home and swing by the beach. Sometimes there was a run. What that means is the bass and salmon are after the bait fish, like the anchovies or sardines, and the pelicans were flying from above them. Every once in a while, the pelican would just dive headfirst into the water. Sometimes the surface of the water would be covered with birds, and so the baitfish are caught between the birds above and the striped bass and salmon below. The fisherman had but to cast a lure anywhere near the birds, and the fish will think it's a bait fish.

I was driving by one day, and I saw the birds diving all over the place. Every fishermen had at least one large striped bass. Some of the fisherman had two. The fish were so big, the fisherman couldn't carry them both. So they would drag one for a short distance, then go back to get the other fish that they had caught. When I saw this, I didn't have my fishing rod and reel with me. So all I could do was watch. I remembered that I teamed up with a group of guys at work that were going out on a party boat. The fishing boat was about 135 feet long. It's destination was the Faraline Islands. We were instructed to drop our lines over the side of the boat, sometimes 50 feet, sometime about 30 feet deep depending on what structures the boat was floating over. We didn't use bait, just skirted hooks with different color skirts, like green, yellow, red, etc. I caught the largest fish in my life. It was a large red snapper. I caught some other smaller fish, and oh did they taste good. Some people on the boat caught big lingcod up to about thirty pounds or more.

I remember learning a dangerous lesson while fishing on the shore of the beach. I bought some chest waders. I thought they would help with the cold water on the beach. What I didn't know was that when you step into the water from the beach's shoreline, you never know how deep the water is. Well, I had my fishing rod in my hands, preparing to make a long cast. I stepped forward in the water. My foot didn't find the bottom. Instead, I got caught in surging water. I think it was called a riptide. So instead of my foot being an anchor, the water picked it up, and I went down. The water sealed the top of my waders, preventing me from escaping from them. My feet were just balloons, and as the water flowed out from the shore, I flowed with it. The only thing that prevented me from going further was the end of my fishing rod. I jammed it into the sand. It acted as a brake, slowing my sliding into the deeper water. As the rest of the water flowed past me, I was finally able to strengthen my grip on the sand. Thank God, I will never do that again.

While attending a large convention at the Moscone Convocation Center in San Francisco, we met a deacon and his wife. We just hit it off right away and became lifelong friends. While talking with him, I discovered that he was a Christian businessman and was devoted to his family and church. He had a bus company and loved to go fishing. We planned a fishing trip, and the rest is history. I was quite impressed with the way that he conducted his business. They would begin the workday with prayer and openly sought God's will for the business. Needless to say, God responded. He rewards those who diligently seeks Him. Today that business is one of the largest around in the Bay Area. But back then, it was a fledgling of a company.

I remember visiting the office in the beginning. The office consisted of an old dilapidated bus hull. The seats had been removed to make room for a simple desk and a few chairs. Now it covers over a city block, all praise to God. Well, back to fishing. We went in his boat and were fishing for sturgeon. There were three of us fishing, and it was so comical. It was me, this deacon, and his brother-in-law. When a fish was hooked, a sturgeon, they were instructing each other on how to land the fish, what tools to use; it was a circus watching them. All I could do was laugh hysterically. But they were very efficient and did land the sturgeon. It was a good-size fish. We each got equal portions, although I didn't feel that I had done any of the work. On another occasion, it was just the deacon and myself. After fishing a while, I was tired and my fishing pole was baited and set up. I took a nap. When I woke up a while later, the deacon was up waiting for me to wake up and had one of Charles Stanley's books in his hand to discuss. If you don't know Charles Stanley, he is a pastor of a large church, a noted speaker and preacher. He has an unusual gift of expounding the Word. We have had many hours of gleaning the Word from his teachings, but now we were fishing.

"For with God nothing shall be impossible" (Luke 1:37 KJV).

What I learned was that the deacon, his family, and his wife's family had many gifts, among which was the gift of hospitality. It was a common practice to find them surrounded by kids and young adults every Sunday after church. They would usually be at a restaurant and hosting everyone. The warmth, love, and devotion to all was always present. I feel honored to know them. Through the countless hours that I have spent with the deacon either alone or with his family, I can say that I have been helped spiritually, as they poured out God's love to me. What a family. Oh, by the way, their names are being withheld to protect their identity.

During this time, I was active pursuing music ministry. I played for a number of churches, sometimes more than one at a time. On Sunday, I would usually play for my home church. In the afternoon and evening, I would usually play at a different church venue. I loved to get lost in worship and let the Spirit use me however He saw fit.

I was invited to join a choir as the musician for the San Francisco Senior Citizen Escort Choir. It was funded by the San Francisco Police Department's budget for community activities. It was a unique idea, and it funded a Christ-centered activity. We were given lots of recognition, and Diane Feinstein, the mayor of San Francisco, declared a Lyrics and Lace Day for us. We were showcased at the San Francisco War Memorial Opera House. It was the first time that I played a twelve-feet-long grand piano. The sound was great. We were given two funded trips. The first trip was a twelve-day trip to Jamaica. We sang in historic churches; one was over one hundred years old. We toured the Island from Montego Bay to Kingston, and so much more. Our schedule was quite full. Our next trip was to Washington D.C. We were accompanied by congressmen, John and Phillip Burton. We were able to sing in the White House. We were to have a brief meeting with President Jimmy Carter, but he was called out to survey a recent tornado in Florida. We were the invited guest choir for a political function in Sacramento, California. Jesse Jackson was the keynote speaker. For all of this, I give God the praise for granting us favor.

Then I met Renee Joseine Jefferson. This part of the story has been told; see earlier chapters. But there is a part of the beginning story I would like to tell. When we first met, I was smitten. She was just so radiant. Her eyes would seem to change colors from a sandy brown to what appeared to be a shade of purple gray. When I told her later, she would just laugh at me. Well, when we went out, I held her hand, and she said that I was measuring her fingers for the ring. I told her that I was looking to see if she had piano fingers. She told me this later too. She went to her oldest sister to ask for advice about me.

She said she felt that I was moving too fast. The next time we talked, she said that she thought that we should be friends. Well, there was a small lake in San Francisco Daly City called Lake Merced. We, my sister and others, would exercise by walking around it. It is a little over one mile, depending on which path that you take. I usually walk it one time. But the day that Renee said that she thought that we should be friends, I walked it twice, and I still wasn't tired. After three days of silence, we decided that it was more than just a friendship. We were married a few months later.

Living in Redding, Going to Bethel Church

Part of this story has been told in an earlier chapter. But after we had read Randy Clark's book, *There Is More*, we did attend a seminar at Bethel Church. We were richly blessed, beyond our wildest imaginations. So, our fleece to the Lord was when we both retire, we had two places in mind to live. Vacaville and go to the Mission Church or move to Redding, California and go to Bethel Church. We were leaning toward Redding, but we agreed that the place that we could find a house to buy, that would be the place. So we tried looking in Vacaville and the surrounding area. We were not able to find a suitable place. So we began our search in Redding. My wife looked online and saw a house that she really liked right away. We contacted a Realtor in Redding and scheduled a weekend to come up and look. In one day, we found our home after looking at about five other homes. So that was our answer. We not only made and offer, it was accepted the same day.

So we, like so many others, had arrived in Redding and were excited and were in awe with what God was going to do with our lives. My wife and I, arrived at Bethel and immediately began the classes to become members. Every class and seminar has been enlightening and full and rich with spiritual fodder. From Deeper

Life, Fire Starters, the Healing rooms, and Diamond Fellowship, to every Sunday service, I find strength and fullness in God's Word. My goal was to not only attend, but also be active and participate in every facet. I believe that God didn't send me here to sit down and watch, but as it is written, "But as it is written, Eye hath not seen, nor ear heard, neither have entered into the heart of man, the things which God hath prepared for them that love him" (1 Cor. 2:9 KJV).

Lord, You said if I told you, would you believe it? If I showed you, would you receive it? What if I took you where there is more than you could understand, more than you could comprehend? I just want you to know that I am God. And I say if You told me, Lord, I will believe it. If You showed me, Lord, help me to receive it. Lord, please take me there. Please take me where there is more than I could understand, more than I could comprehend. Lord, I know that You are God.

Purpose

The purpose of this book is to encourage everyone to be sensitive to God and His voice. He does speak in so many ways to send His love, guidance, and support into our lives. In the Bible, He used the gentle voice to the loud clap of thunder. To know God's heart is to know that He wants us all to receive all of the things that He has for us. Although He has used birds, flies, lice, fire, plants, worms, storms, or the gentle dove, they all were to express His purpose. I pray that His truth be revealed to you through the love and grace of our Saviour, Jesus Christ.

Book 2: Fears, Phobias, and Other Distorted Things

God does not give us the spirit of fear but power, love, and a sound mind. Every day it seem that there is another thing mentioned either in the media, radio, television. Or just listening to people's conversation that is initiated with fear; fear of a different substance if contact was made long ago now bring fear of some disease. The commercials are usually pushing products to shield a person from something harmful. Their solutions involves their services. When I was a young kid, I was afraid of the dark and would cover my head up with heavy blankets and quilts for safety. When my brothers came into the bedroom, I would pull down the covers. I felt safer when they were around. I remember that we lived in a small logging camp, and there were normally sounds of little creatures at night to add to the elements of fear. We didn't have a television, just a family radio. So the source wasn't coming from that. I do remember my brother and I playing games to scare each other. I think that that the darkness just seemed to hold some monsters. My parents were always comforting, especially my mother. I think that many children grow up with unrealistic fears and find ways of shielding them even when they become adults. As I grew up, I discovered that many of our childhood fears and phobias disappear as we gain knowledge and understanding that there was nothing to fear. But if some fears are not dealt with, they can pose a problem later on. Knowing God as our personal Saviour gives us comfort that He will never leave us nor will He forsake us. Therefore, we have no need to fear.

While working in my chosen profession, I was a licensed psychiatric technician at the University of California at San Francisco. We worked with many modalities of treatment. Many of the clients' biggest problems were fear or some kind of phobia, which was usually associated with anxiety or fear of a particular thing. It was futile to just tell them that they should just get rid of their fear and they would be well. Most times, the fears go much deeper than that. Now we know that if we are in Christ, we are a new creature. Behold, old things are passed away and all things are new. Perfect love cast out all fears. My encouragement is for those who are without Christ, come back, you need Him. For it is He who has perfect love, and it is His perfect love that cast out all fears. There is an acronym for fear as being false evidence appearing real. It is not a perfect definition. But there is some truth to it. The number of fears and phobias start with a false premise. If someone had been told that something is real for years, they tend to believe it. There was a study done where a single person in a large group starts to look up to the sky, others will join in. Many times, we as a people will do something to not be singled out from the crowd. This can be a fear of not wanting to have an identity different from everyone else.

"Casting all your cares upon Him for He cares for you. Be sober, be vigilant because your adversary the devil, as a roaring lion, walketh about, seeking whom he may devour: whom resist steadfast in the faith, knowing that the same afflictions are accomplished in your brethren that are in the world" (1 Pet. 5:8-9 KJV).

Fear may be a preventive to receiving blessings from God. It has even been said that the phrase "fear not" is used close to one hundred times in the Bible. When an angelic being is encountered by someone, in the Bible or right now, the first words may be "fear not."

About the Author

Le Brooks was the fourth born of six siblings. He was born in Arizona and then his family moved to Redding, California, where he attended local schools and college. His parents were Christians, and were good role models in showing his family how to live the Christian life. He gave his life to Jesus at the age of twelve and received the Holy Spirit at the age of fifteen. He grew up with a fondness for hunting, fishing, and playing music, specifically the piano and organ. He played the piano and organ for various churches. He got married, and they had twins, Brian and Lanae. This marriage lasted twenty-two years. He then met and married Renee, who became the love of his life. They were inseparable until her death in 2017 of ovarian cancer. Almost two years after losing Renee, he met a lovely woman named Benita Foster at Bethel Church in the Hebrews Café. They became very good friends from the start. Their friendship has grown into a wonderful relationship, and after months of conversation, attending church together and meeting her wonderful family, he felt a tug in his heart, and they married on October 23, 2019. They have been constant companions, and God has blessed their union, and they have grown spiritually and financially. Le loves her and looks forward to spending the rest of his life with her. He remains devoted and loyal to his cause knowing that he was left here for a purpose to fulfill.

CPSIA information can be obtained
at www.ICGtesting.com
Printed in the USA
BVHW092048050422
633050BV00001B/83